KidCaps' Presents

# The Vietnam War:
*A History Just for Kids!*

KidCaps is An Imprint of BookCaps™
www.bookcaps.com

# Table of Contents

# About KidCaps

KidCaps is an imprint of BookCaps™ that is just for kids! Each month BookCaps will be releasing several books in this exciting imprint. Visit are website or like us on Facebook to see more!

Soldiers jump off of a helicopter and run into battle during the Vietnam War[1]

[1] Image source: http://commons.wikimedia.org/wiki/Category:Battles_and_operations_of_the_Vietnam_War

# Introduction

NguyễnVănVien opened his eyes and saw nothing. It was pitch black outside and everything in his house was quiet. His parents and brothers must still be sleeping, so he would have to be careful not to make any noise as he got out of bed. Actually, Vien didn't know why he was awake. It was summertime, so if it was still dark outside then it must be early. Normally he had to wake up with the sun at around 6:30 to get an early start with his chores. As the oldest boy, it was his honor to feed the family chickens and to search for eggs every morning.

As he sat up and put his bare feet onto the cool earth of the floor, Vien was reminded that his family was not rich; they couldn't even afford a floor for the house. But they were one of the few families that could have eggs every day; other families could only afford to eat rice and vegetables, maybe a little bit of fish every now and then. But with sixteen hens and two roosters, the Nguyễn family gathered more eggs each week than they could possibly eat. Although his mother wanted to sell the extra eggs at the market in the nearby village of Con

Thien, his father almost always ended up giving them to one of their hungry neighbors.

Vien listened carefully and noticed that everything was remarkably quiet outside. Normally he could hear the hum of insects from the jungle surrounding his family's house, and sometimes the two roosters would try to out crow each other. But tonight he heard nothing. No crowing, no buzzing, just silence.

Then it began.

The sounds seemed to come from everywhere all at once. He felt like his bed was being lifted from the ground, and the world around had exploded into a million billion fiery pieces. Where moments before there had been blackness and tranquility he now saw bright lights and heard screaming words that he couldn't understand. The blankets under him seemed hot, and he realized that they were on fire. Rolling onto the floor away from his bed he tried to yell for his family, but thick black smoke filled his lungs and made him start coughing. He backed up towards the space where seconds ago a wall had been.

A strong pair of hands grabbed him under his armpits and pulled him out and away from his house. Without even seeing who was holding him Vien starting hitting and kicking. Surely he was being kidnapped by the Northern Communists. He had heard that they liked to take boys around his age, which was twelve, and force them to be a part of their army. But no matter how hard his bare feet clawed at the soft dirt or how fiercely his little fists hit the thick black hands holding him, he was pulled further and further away from his house and family.

To his right, he saw two men arguing. They were both dressed in green, and Vien realized that they must be the Americans he had heard about who had been fighting in the other villages. He hadn't actually seen an American soldier before. One soldier pushed the other and pointed at the house. The second one shook his head and pointed at his chest.

Vien couldn't imagine what they were fighting, and anyways it didn't matter right now. His house was being eaten by the flames, and he thought that he could hear his little brother crying over the roaring fire. The soldier who had dragged him out set him down and went running back towards the fire. But the flames were too hot for him to go in and the water well was way away on the other side of the hill. There was nothing to be done. The fire could not be stopped. His family could not be saved.

Vien got up and started to run to the house, to find his parents and his brothers and to at least try to get them out. But the big same soldier that had carried him before now put his arms out and held Vien back. The heat from the inferno burnt Vien's cheeks as he finally got enough breath to scream out in pain and sadness. The soldier picked him up and carried him away, Vien looking over his soldier and shrieking, crying, not understanding. The other two soldiers were still arguing, and their voices were getting louder and louder. Although Vien could not understand the words, he got the idea. One of the men was responsible for the fire, and the other was mad at him for it. Three more soldiers came from the other side of the house. Vien looked at them with wet eyes, and they looked away. They said something to the big black soldier holding him and then shook their heads. One walked away from the group, put one hand against a tree, and started to throw up in the bushes.

Vien was all alone now. He didn't know what had happened or why, but he was suddenly sure of one thing: he had nobody now. The big soldier holding him put him down onto the ground and knelt before him. His tone was soft as he said something, and Vien could see that the soldier was sad too. He rubbed the top of Vien's head and pointed up to the sky, which was beginning to lighten as the sun rose. At first he didn't see anything but soon he heard a steady *thump thumpthump* and saw a helicopter come up over the horizon. He looked back at the soldier who nodded his head.

As the helicopter lifted a few minutes later, Vien felt strange and sad about what had happened. He felt guilty for enjoying the ride, but a thick knot quickly developed in his stomach as the helicopter went higher and higher. He could see his house, still burning, but he could also see lots of other houses burning on the mountainside. Like stars in the night sky, dozens of fires raged in the dark jungle below. Vien could only imagine how many other boys like him had lost everything. He covered his face with his eyes and wept.

How do you feel when you read the story of NguyễnVănVien? Does it make you sad to read about his suffering and his fear? The truth is that lots of kids just like Vien lost their homes, their families, and even their lives during the Vietnam War. It was a sad time and millions of people's lives were forever changed by it. Have you heard much about the Vietnam War? Do you know someone who fought in it? In this book, we will take a closer look at this war that got the whole world's attention. We will find out what happened to the kids like Vien and why there was so much confusion and even disagreement among the troops fighting in the war. What else can you expect to see in this book?

We will look at what led up to the actual war. Although the United States did not officially start fighting until 1964, there had been conflict and violence in the country of Vietnam for over twenty years, since World War Two. We will learn what led to the United States' involvement and how the fighting began.

Then we will learn about *why* the war happened. Although the war was actually a civil war between the Vietnamese people, it ended up involving soldiers and civilians from China, the Soviet Union, the United States, Laos, and Cambodia. Why did so many people end up fighting? As we will see in this section, each country had its own motive, and its own reasons to get involved.

The following section will tell us more about some of the things that happened during the war itself. We will see the unique tactics used by both sides and whether or not they worked. In one case, the tactic of using statistics would have awful consequences for both sides. We will also see some of the problems faced by the soldiers fighting the war and some of the effects the battle had on average Americans living back in the U.S.

Then we will see what it was like to be a kid back then. Whether you lived in the U.S. or in the middle of the war, you would have had to think about the fighting every day. Would you be surprised to learn that not everyone thought that the war was a good idea? And then the next section will talk about how the war finally ended and then we'll see what happened afterwards. From the effects on the people fighting, on the civilians, and on the countries themselves, the Vietnam War still affects millions of people today.

Are you ready to learn more? While parts of this book may make us a little sad, especially the parts that talk about the violence, try to look at each section from two different viewpoints: what the Americans were thinking and what the Vietnamese people were thinking. At the end of the book, we will ask some tough questions, questions that a lot of people still can't agree on today. They will have to do with whether or not it was right to fight the war and whether or not things could have been done differently.

Keep reading and together we will learn more about the Vietnam War.

# Chapter 1: What Led Up to the Vietnam War?

Although there was fighting in Vietnam for many years, when we talk about "The Vietnam War" we are specifically talking about the time when American soldiers were fighting against Communist forces in Vietnam and its surrounding countries (including Laos and Cambodia). Although there had been American troops and American equipment helping the South Vietnamese fight since 1962, the real war between American soldiers and the Communist troops began in March 1965 and ended in the spring of 1973. But how did American soldiers end up halfway around the globe participating in a small Asian country's civil war? It all started shortly after World War Two ended.

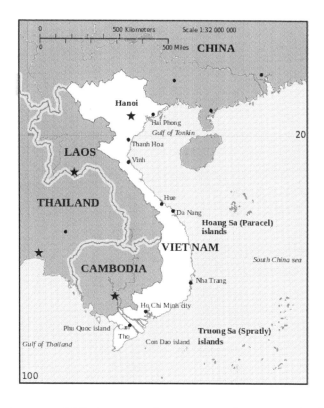

A map of Vietnam and some nearby countries[2]

Ever since the late 1800s, the country of France
had been in control of several countries in
Southeast Asia, including Vietnam. The whole
region was called Indochina, and included the
countries of Vietnam, Laos, and Cambodia.
While the French were busy fighting against the
Germans in Europe during World War Two,

[2] Image source: http://en.wikipedia.org/wiki/Vietnam

Japan aggressively invaded the area and took over some land from Vietnam. The Japanese began to boss around the people who lived there. But when the war ended, and Japan went back to their island, the people of Vietnam decided that they didn't want *anyone* to be in charge of them anymore and began to fight against the French.

The northern part of the country thought that the best thing for Vietnam would be to be an independent Communist country. So a communist political party called the ViệtMinh Party was then organized by a man named Ho Chi Minh. Ho Chi Minh was inspired by the Communist takeovers of China and the Soviet Union, and he thought that the Communist way of life would help his people in Vietnam. During a time when there wasn't enough food to eat because no one had any money to buy it, Ho Chi Minh and his ViệtMinh party broke into the warehouses like Robin Hood and gave the rice they stole to the hungry Vietnamese people. Because he put food on their tables, many Vietnamese citizens began to support the Communist ViệtMinh party. In 1945, he seized the northern city of Hanoi and made it the capital of a new country, the Democratic republic of Vietnam (North Vietnam).

The fighting got worse and worse between the Vietnamese and the French, and the French were finally defeated at the Battle of Dien Bien Phu that ended on May 7, 1954. The French had few troops after all of the violence of World War Two, so although they tried to hold onto their power in Vietnam the fighting obviously didn't go too well for them. The international community decided that the French should leave Vietnam in the hands of the Vietnamese. The country would be temporarily divided into two halves, North and South, with a border at the 17$^{th}$ Parallel. It was also decided that the country would have a special election in 1956 to decided how best to reunite the two halves.

The French obeyed and left the country in 1954 but made sure that the southern part stayed under the control of French-educated Emperor BảoĐại. Although the emperor had been around for a while, he was not immensely popular. NgôĐìnhDiệm, a politician who became popular with the United States because he hated Communists, became the Prime Minister and then forced the emperor to leave the country. A special election was held, and in 1955, NgôĐìnhDiệm became the first president of the Republic of Vietnam (South Vietnam).

The country was now officially split into two halves, north and south, with two different leaders who had different ways of thinking and yet who both wanted the country to be united under one government. The problem was that everyone couldn't agree on what sort of government that should be. Can you see how things were starting to get complicated in Vietnam?

What kind of President was NgôĐìnhDiệm? Well, he was the sort of man who did everything possible to get his way, even if it meant breaking the rules and hurting other people. While the United States liked him because he hated Communism, they quickly realized that President NgôĐìnhDiệm was a brutal dictator. Instead of trying to unite his country peacefully as the international community had told him to, he cancelled the vote and began to kill everyone that did not agree with him. Instead of letting the people decide wither they wanted a communist government or a democratic government, he rounded up everyone who supported the North Vietnamese Communists and had them put in jail, tortured, and killed. It is believed that soon after becoming president NgôĐìnhDiệm killed over 100,000 people this way.

NgôĐìnhDiệm was also distrusting of anyone who wasn't related to him, and his government was corrupt. That means that a lot of people didn't do their jobs and that they kept lots of money for themselves instead of sharing it with the poor citizens who they were supposed to be helping. As a result of seeing so much suffering, groups of citizens in South Vietnam got together and formed an organization called the National Liberation Front (the NLF). In Vietnamese, the name of this organization was called Việtcộng. The Việtcộng, or NLF, was supposedly made up of both communist soldiers from the north and democratic soldiers from the south. They were united by the common goal of uniting Vietnam together and getting rid of bad leaders. However, the United States felt that the Việtcộng didn't represent all of the Vietnamese people and that it was only a tool for the Northern Communists.

The fighting between the Việtcộng and the South Vietnam military got more and more frequent during the late 1950s. From 1957-1959, the fighting escalated from small skirmishes to full out battles between large groups of soldiers. Back in 1954, President Dwight D. Eisenhower had promised to help the South out as much he could without actually doing any of the fighting, so he ended up sending over 900 soldiers as "advisors" to help the South fight their war against the North.

In January of 1961 John F. Kennedy became President of the United States. It was clear to everyone that the situation was getting more and more serious in Vietnam and that the South was likely to be taken over by the Communist North. Because the U.S. Government had promised to help the South Vietnamese government, President Kennedy was urged by his advisors to send more people to Vietnam. By 1962, some 9,000 American troops were in South Vietnam to provide training to Vietnamese troops there, and by 1963, there were 16,000 troops stationed there. There was continued fighting between the North and the South, but the Americans saw no reason to get any more involved than they already were.

In November of 1963, all of that changed.

On November 2, NgôĐìnhDiệm was assassinated by a group of his fellow countrymen, and less than three weeks later President John F. Kennedy was also assassinated. Two of the primary figures in the struggle to keep South Vietnam out of the hands of the Communist forces had died, and there was absolute chaos in both governments. Although President Kennedy had signed an order to withdraw troops from Vietnam his successor, President Lyndon B. Johnson, expanded the number of troops and work to be done there.

Lyndon B. Johnson was sworn in as President on November 22, 1963[3]

There was no one leader to replace NgôĐìnhDiệm in South Vietnam, and several more attempts were made by various groups trying to take control of the situation. Finally, General Nguyen Khanh took control in 1964.

[3] Image source: http://en.wikipedia.org/wiki/Lyndon_B._Johnson

Although he increased the amount of troops in Vietnam, President Johnson did not see the situation there as important, and he preferred to focus his attention of other matters. But soon he would be forced to rethink how he was dealing with this small country in Southeast Asia.

On August 2, 1964, the USS *Maddox*, a United States destroyer, was patrolling the waters off the coast of North Vietnam in an area called the Gulf of Tonkin when suddenly it reported that it had been fired upon by three North Vietnamese torpedo boats. They fired back, sinking one of the North Vietnamese ships, and several planes went out to investigate and protect the *Maddox*. Two days later, on August 4, there were more reports of American ships narrowly dodging North Vietnamese torpedoes.

Now President Johnson had to decide what to do. Instead of simply provide advice and guidance to South Vietnamese troops fighting a civil war, American soldiers had been fired upon. They had been trying to maintain internationally recognized territory, and now it looked like the North was becoming more aggressive than ever.

On August 5, President Johnson went before Congress and gave a speech that included the following words:

"Our policy in southeast Asia has been consistent and unchanged since 19554. I summarized it on June 2 in four simple propositions:

1. America keeps her word. Here as elsewhere, we must and shall honor our commitments.

2. The issue is the future of Southeast Asia as a whole. A threat to any nation in that region is a threat to all, and a threat to us.

3. Our purpose is peace. We have no military, political, or territorial ambitions in the area.

4. This is not just a jungle war, but a struggle for freedom on every front of human activity. Our military and economic assistance to South Vietnam and Laos in particular has the purpose of helping these countries to repel aggression and strengthen their independence.

The threat to the free nations of Southeast Asia has long been clear. The North Vietnamese regime has constantly sought to take over South Vietnam and Laos. This Communist regime has violated the Geneva accords for Vietnam. It has systematically conducted a campaign of subversion, which includes the direction, training, and supply of personnel and arms for the conduct of guerrilla warfare in South Vietnamese territory."[4]

In that important speech, called the Gulf of Tonkin Resolution, President Johnson asked for the support of Congress in giving more aid to South Vietnam. Although there was no specific mention of war, the President knew that Congress would let him do whatever he thought was appropriate.

As more American troops arrived in Vietnam, the number of supporters of the Việtcộng also increased, numbering about 100,000 by the end of 1964. The Việtcộng saw more American troops as a threat to the independence of Vietnam were ready to fight against any new soldiers that arrived. On March 2, 1965, some barracks (the place where soldiers live) were attacked and the U.S. responded by bombing the enemy. Six days later 3,500 Marines were sent to South Vietnam to fight.

The Vietnam War had officially begun.

---

[4] Quotation source: http://www.pbs.org/wgbh/amex/vietnam/psources/ps_tonkingulf.html

22

# Chapter 2: Why Did the Vietnam War Happen?

When you look at that question, "Why did the Vietnam War happen," you might think that there is a simple answer. However as we will see in this section, the Vietnam War was fought largely due to miscommunication. The Vietnamese didn't understand what the Americans wanted, and the Americans didn't understand what the Vietnamese wanted. And the end result was that over three million people from many different countries died. As we talk about the "why" of the Vietnam War, don't be afraid to ask yourself or any adults you know some of the tough questions, like "Did this war have to happen?"and "Could it have been avoided?" Let's learn more.

We will start by looking at the war and the events leading up to it through the eyes of the Vietnamese people. Do you remember why Ho Chi Minh formed the ViệtMinh Party in the first place? While he and his partners certainly agreed with the Communist way of thinking and doing things, their party name specifically mentioned their greater goal. The name

"ViệtMinh" was short for "Việt Nam ĐộcLậpĐồng Minh Hội", which in English means "The League for the Independence of Vietnam". The reason that Ho Chi Minh and the others formed their Communist political party was to fight for an independent Vietnam. After decades of being bossed around first by the French and then by the Japanese, the Vietnamese people wanted to rule for themselves.

When NgôĐìnhDiệm became President and started to treat his fellow Vietnamese cruelly, we saw that a group called the Việtcộng was formed. In English, the name Việtcộng meant National Liberation Front. Because "liberation" has to do with freeing something that is being held like a prisoner, we can see again that the Vietnamese people were not necessarily interested in Communism or Democracy; they simply wanted their country to be free. As the United States began to support different leaders (first NgôĐìnhDiệm and then others). many Vietnamese felt like it was history repeating itself all over again. They felt that foreign nations were coming in again to tell them how to run their country.

Now imagine how many of the common Vietnamese citizens felt as they saw more and more troops come from the United States and move into their neighborhoods and villages. Do you think that they would have been happy to see these strange men dressed in green uniforms or would they have been afraid? The truth is that instead of seeing the American soldiers as people who were there to help them to restore the peace, most Vietnamese (including those from the South) viewed the Americans as big bullies who just wanted to take over Vietnam and to become the new bosses. For that reason, many chose to fight against the American soldiers.

This way of thinking can be seen in a conversation years later between two of the important men of the Vietnam War: U.S. Secretary of Defense Robert McNamara and Vietnamese Foreign Minister NguyễnCơThạch.

Robert McNamara (on the right) with President Johnson during an important meeting[5]

During an interview years later, Robert McNamara mentioned how surprised he was when he learned what the Vietnamese had been fighting for all along. He said:

> "In the case of Vietnam, we didn't know them well enough to empathize. And there was total misunderstanding as a result. They believed that we had simply replaced the French as a colonial power, and we were seeking to subject South and North Vietnam to our colonial interests, which was absolutely absurd. And we, we saw Vietnam as an element of the Cold War. Not what they saw it as: a civil war.
>
> There aren't many examples in which you bring two former enemies together, at the highest levels, and discuss what might have been. I formed the hypothesis that each of us could have achieved our objectives without the terrible loss of life. And I wanted to test that by going to Vietnam. The former Foreign Minister of Vietnam, a wonderful man named Thạch said, "You're totally wrong. We were

fighting for our independence. You were fighting to enslave us."

"Do you mean to say it was not a tragedy for you, when you lost 3 million 4 hundred thousand Vietnamese killed, which on our population base is the equivalent of 27 million Americans? What did you accomplish? You didn't get any more than we were willing to give you at the beginning of the war. You could have had the whole damn thing: independence, unification."

"Mr. McNamara, You must never have read a history book. If you'd had, you'd know we weren't pawns of the Chinese or the Russians. McNamara, didn't you know that? Don't you understand that we have been fighting the Chinese for 1000 years? We were fighting for our independence. And we would fight to the last man. And we were determined to do so. And no amount of bombing, no amount of U.S. pressure would ever have stopped us." "[6]

---

[6] Quotation source: http://www.errolmorris.com/film/fow_transcript.html

Do you understand that important conversation? The Vietnamese Foreign Minister said that the Vietnamese people were fighting for their independence. When they saw the U.S. soldiers come marching in with their guns, they felt the same way as the American colonists did back in 1776 when they saw the British redcoats come marching in with their guns. The Vietnamese thought that they were fighting for their freedom.

But what did the Americans think that they were fighting for?

The Americans thought that they were fighting to contain Communism, to keep it from spreading any further than it already had. After watching the Soviet Union and China be overthrown by Communist soldiers, the American government worried that other countries might become Communist too, and that all of them would get together and form a super nation that would start another world war and take over the world. Like dominoes all lined up in a row, they thought that if one country in Southeast Asia became Communist then others might also. President Johnson, in several private phone calls to Defense Secretary Robert McNamara, explained how he thought something like that could happen:

"I would say that we have a commitment to Vietnamese freedom. We could pull out of there, the dominoes would fall, and that part of the world would go to the Communists."

"We have declared war on tyranny and aggression. If this little nation goes down the drain and can't maintain her independence, ask yourself what's going to happen to all these other little nations."[7]

This theory, called the "Domino Theory" was made popular earlier by President Eisenhower and continued to affect the decisions made by presidents throughout the Korean and Vietnam Wars. By sending troops to fight in Vietnam, the Americans felt like they were genuinely fighting against Communism. And because China and the Soviet Union were giving supplies to the North Vietnamese, for the Americans this war turned into part of the Cold War with the Soviets.

---

[7]                  Quotation                  source:
http://www.errolmorris.com/film/fow_transcript.html

Like dominos in a line that fall one after another, President Johnson was afraid that lots of countries would become Communist if Vietnam was allowed to fall[8]

Can you see how this confusion totally changed the war? What do you think would have happened if the people involved stopped for a few minutes to try and figure out why the other side was acting a certain way or why they were doing certain things? Do you think that so many people would have died?

[8] Image source: http://insureblog.blogspot.com/2012/07/dominos-part-deux.html

Defense Secretary Robert McNamara explained that the very cause of the United States sending more troops to Vietnam to fight, the Gulf of Tonkin Resolution, was also the result of a big misunderstanding. It turns out that U.S. ships were not attacked by North Vietnamese boats on August 4 as they had told everyone. McNamara said:

> "It was just confusion, and events afterwards showed that our judgment that we'd been attacked that day was wrong. It didn't happen. And the judgment that we'd been attacked on August 2nd was right. We had been, although that was disputed at the time. So we were right once and wrong once.

> Ultimately, President Johnson authorized bombing in response to what he thought had been the second attack. It hadn't occurred, but that's irrelevant to the point I'm making here. He authorized the attack on the assumption it had occurred, and his belief that it was a conscious decision on the part of the North Vietnamese political and military leaders to escalate the conflict and an indication they would not stop short of winning.

We were wrong, but we had in our minds a mindset that led to that action. And it carried such heavy costs. We see incorrectly or we see only half of the story at times."[9]

As Robert McNamara said, there was a certain "mindset", or way of thinking, that many people in the United States government had at that time. They wanted to fight Communism, and they wanted to win a war. After having lost the Battle of the Bay of Pigs in Cuba and after having problems with the Soviets' building a wall in Berlin, the United States felt like it had a lousy reputation in the world. They were looking for a chance to be the heroes again, and when the civil war in Vietnam broke out and it looked like the Communist party might win, the United States thought it was their chance to ride in and save the day.

But as we saw earlier, the Vietnamese did not think they needed help from anyone else. They wanted to decide for themselves how to run the country and anyone who got involved would have a fight on their hands. The Vietnam War was actually just a civil war, but because of miscommunication and strong opinions, it

---

[9]                     Quotation                       source:
http://www.errolmorris.com/film/fow_transcript.html

quickly became a terrible conflict that would eventually kill over three million people. Do you think it could have gone differently? What would you have done if you had been there?

# Chapter 3: What Happened During the Vietnam War?

The Vietnam War was a confusing time for almost everyone involved. As we already mentioned, the two sides didn't understand each other and weren't exactly sure what their enemy wanted to achieve. But the Vietnam War saw some interesting things happen for the first time ever on the battlefield. There was a focus on **attrition** and not on gaining more territory; there were **problems within the ranks** of the American soldiers, and many people back in the United States thought that the war created too much **controversy**. Let's look at each of those special circumstances one by one.

First, the United States did not have the same goals as most armies did during previous wars: to try to move their men forward and to conquer more land. From the very beginning, American soldiers were sure that the North Vietnamese were remarkably few in number. So instead of moving forward into North Vietnam to fight them, the Americans decided on a war of

**attrition**. Attrition has to do with losing something a little bit at a time. The idea was that American soldiers would form a kind of "wall" in South Vietnam and then let the North Vietnamese come to them. As time went by, the Americans would win most of the battles, and the North Vietnamese would eventually run out of soldiers and ammunition to fight the war. In the meantime, the South Vietnamese would take care of the Việtcộng in their territory, behind the "wall" of Americans.

The first phase of the plan was initiated in March of 1965 and was called Operation Rolling Thunder. Along with stopping the movement of soldiers from the North to the South, Operation Rolling Thunder had the goal of making sure that North Vietnam stopped supported the Việtcộng fighters in the South. Lots of different types of bombs were dropped on North Vietnam to make this happen. There were bombs to destroy anti-aircraft missiles and bombs for destroying military targets and even bombs for oil storage warehouses. But no matter how many thousands of pounds of explosives were dropped in North Vietnam, the Americans didn't see any real difference. The North Vietnamese had prepared well and were even able to set traps for the flying bombers and shoot lots of them down.

As the focus began to move more and more onto the ground war that the soldiers were fighting in South Vietnam, different types of bombs were used. During a special plan called Operation Ranch Hand, strong chemicals were sprayed over parts of South Vietnam. The chemicals would kill all of the plants in the area.

A United States helicopter spraying Agent Orange over the jungles of Vietnam[10]

Why did the United States want to kill the plants in South Vietnam? Well, the soldiers simply weren't used to having to fight and move through so many plants. It gave the Việtcộng so many places to hide and made sure that they

10 Image source: http://commons.wikimedia.org/wiki/File:US-Huey-helicopter-spraying-Agent-Orange-in-Vietnam.jpg

had plenty of food. So by killing the plants, the Americans hoped that the Việtcộng wouldn't be able to hide anymore, the battles would be easier, and that eventually they would have to give up because of not having food.

The Americans also hoped to force most of the Vietnamese to go away from the war zone and into the large cities. Why? Well, as we will see later, the Việtcộng did not wear military uniforms: they looked just like everyone else. Because the soldiers couldn't always tell who was an innocent civilian and who was a trained soldier waiting to kill them, it made the stress levels high. The chemicals dropped on the jungles should make all that easier.

Unfortunately, the chemicals that were dropped (including one called Agent Orange) had terrible side effects. Any Vietnamese people were born with diseases, many babies died in their mother's wombs, and the American soldiers themselves got cancer from Agent Orange after the war had finished. Although they may have helped the war effort a little bit, Agent Orange and the other chemicals dropped on the jungles of South Vietnam did a lot of harm to both the Vietnamese people and to the American soldiers.

The whole strategy of the war had to do with **attrition**, because the Americans believed that the North Vietnamese and the Việtcộng were small in number and that the war wouldn't last too long. However as the fighting went on, more and more Việtcộng kept popping up in South Vietnam and more and more North Vietnamese kept fighting strong for their country. In other words, no matter how many people died in the fighting, there were always more soldiers coming onto the battlefields. The idea of attrition wasn't working.

This was made especially clear on January 30, 1968. Three years after the bombing and fighting had started, the Americans were shocked when they saw a huge, well-organized attack carried out by the North Vietnamese in multiple cities. Called the Tet Offensive ("Tet" was the Vietnamese word for the new year) it showed that the North Vietnamese and the Việtcộng weren't going anywhere and that they were still strong, still organized, and still ready to fight.

The city of Saigon was attacked severely during the Tet Offensive[11]

In other words, after three years, the Americans were still not anywhere near to winning the war. The strategy of using **attrition** to win the war was not working.

---

[11] Image source: http://commons.wikimedia.org/wiki/File:SaigonTet1968.jpg

Other important factors in the Vietnam War were the **problems faced by the American soldiers** themselves. As we mentioned earlier, the Vietnam War was unlike all previous wars. The enemy did not wear special uniforms or march together in large armies. They dressed the same as the innocent civilians and would often hide with civilian families pretending to be just another villager. Then when the American soldiers weren't looking they would shoot them down or throw a grenade.

The American soldiers learned to not trust any Vietnamese people that they saw. They thought that the only way to stay alive was to shoot first and ask questions later. As a result, a lot of innocent people died. But it got even worse. As part of their strategy of attrition, the U.S. government focused a lot on the numbers. They wanted to know how many bombs were dropped, how many bullets were fired, and how many enemy soldiers were killed. The American forces on the ground felt a lot of pressure to shoot more people so that the reports looked better, and so they often threw grenades, used flamethrowers, and shot their guns without making sure that the targets were actually enemies, and not innocent villagers.

A tragedy in the South Vietnamese city of Mỹ Lai is a good example of what was happening on the ground during the Vietnam War. On March 16, 1968, American soldiers marched into this small village to check for Việtcộng soldiers. They had been told that all of the villagers would be at the market buying food and that anyone who was still in the village when the Americans arrived must be Việtcộng fighters. The soldiers went in ready to fight.

After suffering at the hands of the North Vietnamese and the Việtcộng fighters a few weeks before during the Tet Offensive, the American soldiers wanted revenge, and wanted to make sure that no more attacks like that could happen again. Their commanders told them that everyone that they came across was sure to be either a Communist or a Communist supporter. And when the soldiers asked about women and children, they were told that *everyone* in that village was a potential threat, even the women and children.

When they entered the village in the morning, the soldiers looked for hiding soldiers in the houses of the elderly villagers. A few villagers were shot, and that made the soldiers start to go kind of crazy. They started shooting animals and people and killing them with grenades and bayonets. They pushed groups of people together into ditches and shot them with machine guns. Women and children were shot and shoved into ditches. When an American helicopter pilot saw what was happening he landed his helicopter between his fellow soldiers and the Vietnamese villagers who were running for their lives and rescued the Vietnamese villagers, who ended up being a group of women, children, and old men.

When they later investigated what had happened at Mỹ Lai, there were no weapons, no young soldiers, and no threat of any kind. In other words, those American soldiers had killed all of those Vietnamese villagers for nothing: they were South Vietnamese supporters who the Americans were supposed to be helping. Because of poor communication, frustration over the difficult war, and an incorrect mindset, 347 innocent Vietnamese citizens died that day.

This is a picture taken of some of the My Lai citizens who were later killed during the massacre[12]

[12] Image source: http://commons.wikimedia.org/wiki/File:My_Lai_massacre_woman_and_children.jpg

The soldiers were fighting a difficult war, and incidents like this one (which came to be called the Mỹ Lai Massacre) made their job even harder. More Vietnamese joined the Việtcộng fighters as they saw the Americans as dangerous bullies who wanted to take away their freedom.

As the war kept progressing, the U.S. government began to wonder whether or not it could be won. They began to wonder whether or not they should keep sending over troops and equipment. All this doubt made the soldiers feel like they were risking their lives every day for nothing and some even began to feel like they were fighting a pointless war. During the final years of the Vietnam War, soldiers started to use drugs, became more violent, deserted the Army, and would even kill their superior officers on purpose. It was a sad time both for Americans and for the Vietnamese.

Another important circumstance that made the Vietnam War unique was that back in the United States, the Vietnam War had created a lot of **controversy**. Although at first a large number of Americans agreed that it was a good idea to send troops to help the Vietnamese fight the Communists, as time went by it started to look like the whole thing had been a huge mistake. Groups of protestors began to demonstrate against the war and to make signs and shout about their opinions on college campuses across the country. Thousands of people marched in Washington D.C. asking the President to end the war. As more and more American soldiers came back and were interviewed about what the war was like, less Americans supported it.

The protests started to divide the country into two halves: those who supported the war and those who didn't. The two sides couldn't understand each other and often ended up fighting between themselves. Some of the college campus protests turned deadly. On May 4, 1970, at Kent State University in Ohio, student protestors who were speaking out against the war and the terrible violence against the Vietnamese people were shot at by National Guard soldiers. Four students were killed, and nine more were wounded.

National Guard soldiers shot tear gas and bullets at the Kent State protestors[13]

All across the country, students went on strike and hundreds of colleges and universities shut down. The country now had to make a decision as to what they were going to do about the war in Vietnam. Never before had the nation become so deeply divided about an issue, and never before had Americans killed Americans over a war that was happening thousands of miles away on the other side of the world.

As more reports surfaced about the awful behavior of American soldiers, many also learned about how President Nixon ordered illegal bombing raids on and an invasion of Vietnam's neighbor Cambodia. This only made the protests increase in size and scope, and President Nixon began secretly recording conversations in order to find out who was the on revealing confidential information. This habit would later get him in trouble during something called the Watergate scandal.

By the early 1970s, things were looking bad in Vietnam, bad in the United States, and bad in the White House. Something had to change.

---

[13] Image source: http://www.kentstate1970.org/

# Chapter 4: What Was It Like to Be a Kid During the Vietnam War?

After seeing all of the sad things that happened during the Vietnam War, can you imagine being a kid back then? In the introduction, we saw the story of NguyễnVănVien. The truth is that there were many kids just like his who lost their families, their homes, and even their lives. Because of soldiers who acted crazy, because of miscommunications, and because of accidents, thousands and thousands of Vietnamese civilians died at the hands of American soldiers.

If you were a kid living in Vietnam, you would probably have been scared the whole time. Not only was there a civil war going on, which was bad enough, but now there were foreign troops dropping bombs, throwing grenades, and shooting guns in your home country. If you were a kid, especially if you were a boy, you would be afraid that someday one of those soldiers might get confused and shoot you because they thought that you were a soldier. Or you might be afraid to go to sleep just in case the enemy came at night and attacked your village.

Just as the Americans were confused about whom their friends were and whom their enemies were, the Vietnamese themselves also didn't always know whom to trust. The kids often got stuck in the middle and were scared of everyone. Worse yet, they often didn't understand what was going on. They weren't the only ones who didn't know why the Americans were killing the Vietnamese.

Back in the United States, American kids watched their older brothers and neighbors go off to war; and they saw how some of them never came home. Over 50,000 young American soldiers died in Vietnam during the war and it made a lot of families sad. Can you imagine watching the news every night and seeing reports of the fighting? Can you imagine going to the funerals of guys you knew and watching their parents cry? Do you think that you would have understood everything that was going on? Would you have agreed with it?

Kids in the U.S. saw the world around them get divided into two groups: those who supported the war and those who didn't. But sometimes, families were divided into two groups also. Mothers and fathers got into arguments about the war, and kids disagreed with parents. It was a scary time, a time when lots of people fought and argued and said mean things. Also, imagine what it would be like to see the protestors. Protestors often marched down the streets so everyone could see them, but unlike other parades where everyone was smiling, these protest marches often had a lot of yelling, and some ended with people on the ground, injured and crying.

Being a kid back then (whether in the United States or in Vietnam) would have been scary and sometimes it would have seemed like the world was losing its mind.

# Chapter 5: How Did the Vietnam War End?

Most wars end with a huge battle or with parades or with a big victory. But the Vietnam War didn't end like that at all. As time went by, the United States government saw that the war could not be won. There were too many enemy soldiers, too many Americans were dying, and the county no longer supported the war effort. Then, the Tet Offensive in 1968 and something similar called the Easter Offensive in 1972 showed that North Vietnamese soldiers and the Việtcộng were nowhere near done fighting.

Secret negotiations were made between the U.S. and North Vietnam, and it was decided to stop sending new soldiers to Vietnam and to bring the soldiers already there back home. On March 29, 1973, the last soldier left Vietnam and returned to the United States.

The Vietnam War had claimed so many lives, yet it ended the same way as it had started: two halves of Vietnam separated at the 17$^{th}$ parallel fighting a civil war. After all the bombs, after all the guns, after all the death and crying, absolutely nothing had changed.

The Americans had been worried about the Communists taking over Southeast Asia if they didn't get involved. So were they right? What actually happened once the American soldiers left?

### What happened after the Vietnam War ended?

After the Vietnam War ended, what Americans had feared would happen actually did happen: South Vietnam was taken over by Communist forces in April, 1975. That same year Laos and Cambodia were also taken over by Communist parties. It looked like the Domino Theory had been right and that Southeast Asia now belonged to the Soviet Union and China.

Only that's not what happened at all.

While those three countries had civil wars and became Communist (Cambodia later changed its mind and became a constitutional monarchy with a King and a Prime Minister) none of them wanted to be under the control of the Soviet Union or China. Even though they chose Communism, they also chose to remain independent from all foreign governments. So even though the Communist ideas spread from one country to another, there was no creation of a new superpower that tried to take over the world; no new international government to threaten global peace.

In other words, the Domino Theory had been wrong. Even if the United States had not gotten involved, and even if all those people wouldn't have died, things probably would have turned out the exact same as they are today.

As the American soldiers who had fought in Vietnam were sent home, they found that no one actually treated them as heroes. Instead of big parades and special dinners in their honor, and visits to the White House, many veterans found that no one was happy with them. Those who had been against the war called them "baby killers" and those who had supported the war were upset with the soldiers and blamed them for not winning it.

Many of the soldiers also suffered from the things that they had seen and heard. About one in every six soldiers suffered some sort of emotional problem after the war. Some people called it "shell shock" and others called it Post Traumatic Stress Disorder (PTSD). It made it hard for soldiers to calm down. Sometimes they felt like they were still at war and that they might be shot at any moment. Because people didn't truly understand a lot about the human brain back then, many made fun of the soldiers and refused to give them jobs. It was not a nice homecoming present.

Over the next few decades international and economic relations were fixed between Vietnam and the United States. In 1982, a beautiful monument was put up in Washington D.C. to honor all those Americans who had died during the Vietnam War. 58,272 names are listed along with the years when they died.

A U.S. Marine looks at the names of fallen soldiers at the Vietnam Veterans Memorial[14]

[14]                          Image                          source:
http://en.wikipedia.org/wiki/Vietnam_Veterans_Memorial

# Conclusion

Although it's kind of sad to learn about the fighting and the suffering of the Vietnam War, it is important for each new generation to learn from the successes and failures of the previous one. Kids learn from parents and parents learn from grandparents. What do you think: was the Vietnam War a success or a failure? A lot of people agree: the Vietnam War should never have happened. Let's review some of the things that we learned in this book.

First, we looked at what led up to the actual war. Although the United States did not officially start fighting until 1964, there had been conflict and violence in the country of Vietnam for over twenty years, since World War Two. The French and the Japanese had dominated Vietnam and the Vietnamese people were tired of it. They decided to fight back, and the Vietnam War happened. We saw how more and more troops we sent to train the South Vietnamese soldiers but how the fighting actually started after the Gulf of Tonkin incident.

Then we learned about *why* the war happened.
Although the war was actually a civil war
between the Vietnamese people, it ended up
involving soldiers and civilians from China, the
Soviet Union, the United States, Laos, and
Cambodia. Why did so many people end up
fighting? As we saw in this section, each country
had its own motive, and its own reasons to get
involved, but most of it had to do with poor
communication. Everybody misunderstood
what the other side wanted. Because of the lack
of communication, friends became enemies and
no one knew who to trust.

The following section told us more about some
of the things that happened during the war
itself. We saw the unique tactic of attrition used
by the Americans and the secret warfare carried
out by the Việtcộng. We also saw how the use of
statistics had awful consequences for both sides
because it made American soldiers more eager to
shoot first and ask questions later. We also saw
some of the problems faced by the soldiers
fighting the war (like not knowing who their
enemy was and who their friend was) and some
of the effects the battles had on average
Americans living back in the U.S., including the
protests at Kent State and other universities.

We also looked at what it was like to be a kid
back then. Whether you lived in the U.S. or in

the middle of the war, you would have had to think about the fighting every day. Were you surprised to learn that not everyone thought that the war was a good idea? And then the next section talked about how the war finally ended. We saw how the U.S. government simply decided to remove the soldiers, realizing that the war could never be won. We then saw what happened afterwards, from the PTSD of the soldiers to the Vietnam Veterans Memorial.

From the effects on the people fighting, on the civilians, and on the countries themselves, the Vietnam War still affects millions of people today. What about you? Did you learn something new about the Vietnam War from reading this book? We sure hope so. And we hope that you have also learned how important it is to ask question. Because the right questions weren't asked before, during, and after the war, a lot of bad decisions were made that led to the suffering of millions of people.

The Vietnam War ended almost forty years ago, but the lessons we can learn will help us far into the future.

41266335R00034